Ancient Myths
The Adventures of Perseus

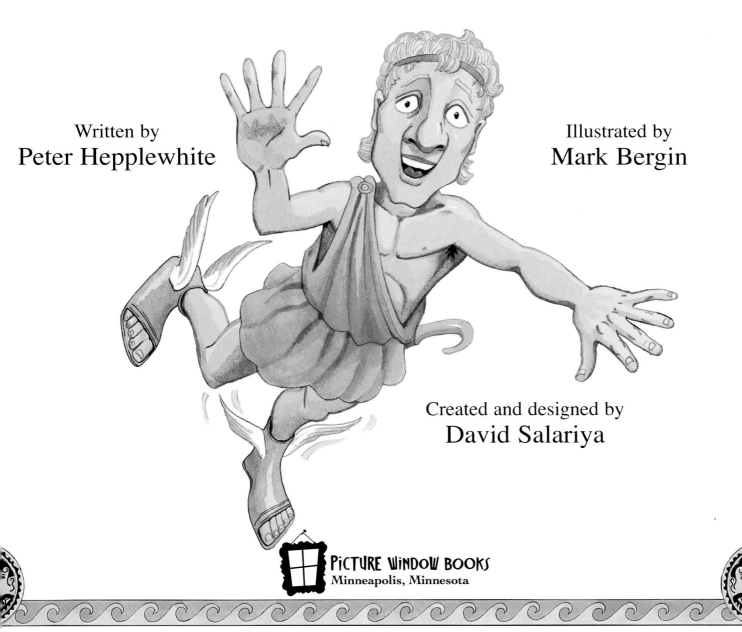

Written by
Peter Hepplewhite

Illustrated by
Mark Bergin

Created and designed by
David Salariya

PICTURE WINDOW BOOKS
Minneapolis, Minnesota

First published in the United States in 2005
by Picture Window Books
5115 Excelsior Boulevard
Suite 232
Minneapolis, MN 55416
1-877-845-8392
www.picturewindowbooks.com

First published in Great Britain in 2004 by Book House,
an imprint of The Salariya Book Company, Ltd.,
25 Marlborough Place, Brighton BN1 1UB
Please visit The Salariya Book Company at
www.salariya.com or *www.book-house.co.uk*

Library of Congress Cataloging-in-Publication Data
Hepplewhite, Peter
The adventures of Perseus/by Peter Hepplewhite, illustrated by
Mark Bergin.
p. cm. – (Ancient myths)
Includes index.
ISBN 1-4048-0901-5 (hardcover)
1. Perseus (Greek mythology) – Juvenile literature. I. Bergin,
Mark. II. Title. III. Series.
BL820.P5H47 2004
398.2'0938'02-dc22
2004001948

Content Adviser: Professor William D. Dyer, Humanities Director,
English Department, Minnesota State University, Mankato

Editors: Michael Ford, Patricia Stockland

About the Author: Peter Hepplewhite is a former history teacher
who now works as Education Officer for Tyne and Wear. Peter
has been a freelance writer for more than 10 years, starting with
school textbooks, before he realized that Greek myths were
more fun.

About the Illustrator: Mark Bergin studied at Eastbourne
College of Art and has illustrated many children's books. He lives
in Bexhill-on-Sea, England, with his wife and three children.

About the Series Creator: David Salariya was born in Dundee,
Scotland. He has illustrated a wide range of books and has created
and designed many new series for publishers worldwide. In 1989,
he established The Salariya Book Company. He lives in Brighton,
England, with his wife, illustrator Shirley Willis, and their son.

For more information on *Perseus,* use FactHound
to track down Web sites related to this book.

1. Go to *www.facthound.com*
2. Type in this book ID: 1404809015
3. Click on the *Fetch It* button.

Your trusty FactHound will fetch the best Web sites for you!

Printed and bound in China. Printed on paper from sustainable forests.

The Adventures of Perseus

Table of Contents

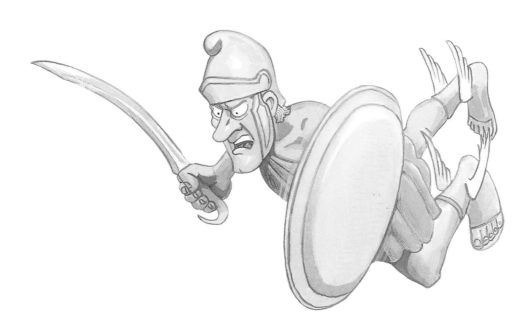

The World of Ancient Mythology

The ancient Greek civilization was one of the greatest the world has witnessed. It spanned nearly 2,000 years, until it was eventually overwhelmed by the Roman Empire in the second century B.C. At its height, the ancient Greek world extended far beyond what we know as modern Greece.

We owe much to the ancient Greeks. They were great scientists, mathematicians, dramatists, and philosophers. They were also brilliant storytellers. Many of the tales they told were in the form of poetry, often thousands of lines long. The Greeks wrote poems on almost every kind of human experience—love, friendship, war, revenge, history, and even simple things like food and daily life. The most famous of the poems that have passed down to us are the epic tales of courage and warfare, where brave heroes struggle and suffer against great odds.

A map showing the ancient Greek mainland, surrounding islands, and territories

What is incredible is that until the eighth century B.C., the Greeks had no recognized form of writing. All of their stories, lengthy as they were, were handed down from generation to generation by word of mouth. The people who passed on these tales were often professional storytellers who would perform in town squares or public theaters. Often, several versions of the same myth existed, depending on who told it and when. What follows is one version of the adventures of Perseus.

If you need help with any of the names, go to the pronunciation guide on page 31.

Introduction

Gather round and hear my story. Is everyone ready? Good. Then I shall begin the tale of Perseus, the slayer of Medusa. But beware, this is not a tale to give you sweet dreams— only nightmares.

We begin in Argos, where King Acrisius was a deeply troubled man. He ruled his kingdom wisely, yet his brother, Proetus, plotted to steal his lands. Faced with such treachery, Acrisius desperately wanted a son —a brave boy to rule Argos after him. Fate had been unkind, however. His only child was a daughter, the beautiful Danae.

Anxiously, the king turned to an oracle for help but was shocked by the prophecy. "You will never have a son," she told him, "and your grandson will kill you." "No!" yelled Acrisius. "You are wrong. I won't let it happen. If my daughter never marries and has no children, I'll be safe."

Gather round and hear my story...

The Birth of Perseus

Acrisius returned to his palace at once. He commanded the guards to lock poor Danae in a tall bronze tower. "Why father?" she sobbed. "What have I done wrong?"

Even the strongest towers can't keep out the gods, though. Mighty Zeus heard Danae's cries and fell in love with her. He came to her as a shower of golden rain, and she became pregnant. Nine months later she gave birth to a son, Perseus. Terrified of what her father might do, she hid the boy in her bedroom, never allowing him to make a noise.

Danae kept her secret for many months until one unlucky day Acrisius heard Perseus crying. Wild with anger, he ordered Danae and his grandson to be locked inside a large wooden chest and set adrift on the Aegean Sea. As the chest floated away, Acrisius hoped they would soon drown.

Danae's prison

King Acrisius imprisoned Danae in a bronze tower —or did he? Other versions of this story tell that Danae was locked in a dungeon with bronze doors, guarded by savage dogs. Either way, her jail wasn't strong enough to keep Zeus away.

Ask the storyteller

Who was Zeus?

Zeus was the most powerful of the Greek gods. He controlled the skies and the weather, striking his enemies with thunderbolts. He had an eye for beautiful girls and had many loves with mortal women.

Rescued!

Dictys the fisherman was sitting by the rocky shore on the island of Seriphos. He was about to cast his net when something caught his eye. Driftwood? No! A chest, bobbing on the waves like a small boat!

Dictys netted the box and hauled it in, eagerly opening the lid. To his surprise, out climbed an exhausted young woman and her child. When he heard Danae's story, Dictys took pity on the castaways and offered them a home. They lived with him for several happy years, and Perseus grew into a sturdy young man, but Danae's good looks were about to get them into trouble again.

One day Polydectes, the king of Seriphos, came to call. He was the brother of Dictys and had fallen in love with Danae. Ignoring her feelings, the king asked her to become his wife. When she refused, he was furious and demanded she obey him. Bristling like a guardian lion, Perseus, now grown-up, warned the king to leave his mother alone.

I need a wife!

Dictys the fisherman

Dictys the fisherman, whose name means "net," was the brother of Polydectes. This didn't make him an important royal prince, though. Monarchs in ancient Greece often ruled small kingdoms, and their relatives might do ordinary work like fishing, sailing, or making pots.

Who was Polydectes?

Polydectes means "much welcoming," but the king of Seriphos didn't live up to his name. He demanded that Danae marry him and wouldn't take no for an answer.

Well, you won't find one here!

Polydectes Issues a Challenge

He hasn't got a chance.

Frightened by Perseus, Polydectes set out to win Danae by trickery. He announced that he would marry another woman, Hippodamia, and invited all the leading men of the island to a banquet. At the feast he asked them to give him a horse as a wedding present. "Seriphos is only a small island," he said, "and I don't want to seem like a beggar compared to other kings who seek the hand of Hippodamia. Will you help me noble Perseus?"

Perseus was poor but proud. "I have no horses or gold, but if you leave my mother alone, I will win whatever gift you seek—even the head of the Gorgon Medusa."

Polydectes grinned in triumph. The fool had put his neck in the noose. He would never survive a battle with Medusa.

"That would please me more than any horse in the world. Go at once, brave Perseus, and may you soon return safely."

Who were the Gorgons?

The three Gorgons were sisters: Stheno, Euryale, and Medusa. Their bodies were covered in scales, their hair squirmed with serpents, and they had tusks like wild boars. The Gorgons were so ugly that anyone who looked them in the eye turned to stone.

Ask the storyteller

Why was Medusa so ugly?

Medusa was once the beautiful lover of Poseidon, god of the sea. One night they slept in a temple dedicated to the goddess Athena, who was so outraged that she changed Medusa into a monster.

Good luck. You'll need it!

A Little Help from the Gods

Overcome with misery, Perseus wandered to a lonely part of Seriphos. "What chance do I have of finding Medusa, let alone killing her?" he sighed. Just as he was about to give up, the goddess Athena and the god Hermes appeared. They had watched his encounter with Polydectes and decided to help.

They took Perseus to the Isle of Samos and showed him pictures of the three Gorgons. "You must be able to recognize Medusa," Athena warned. "She is mortal, but her sisters cannot die. If you attack them, they will kill you." Next they armed Perseus. Hermes gave him a curved crystal sword tough enough to cut through Medusa's scales, while Athena gave him a shield so highly polished that it shone like a mirror. "Use this to pick out your enemy. You can look at her reflection safely, but never look directly into her eyes," the goddess warned.

Athena, warrior goddess

Athena was the guardian of Athens and looked after craftspeople of all kinds. Her father was Zeus, and her birth certainly gave him a pain. Zeus was suffering from violent headaches, so Hermes sent for Hephaestus, the god of blacksmiths. Swinging his great hammer, Hephaestus struck Zeus on his head. Out of the wound jumped Athena—fully grown and fully armed.

Remember, don't look directly at Medusa. Use this shield instead.

Ask the storyteller
Who was Hermes?

Hermes was the son of Zeus and the goddess Maia. When he was still a baby, Hermes stole a herd of cows belonging to Apollo, the god of medicine and music. He made the herd walk backwards so that their tracks left Apollo baffled as he tried to trace them. Seeing Hermes's quick wit, Zeus made him the messenger of the gods and the guardian of roads and travelers.

The All-Seeing Eye

Last of all, Athena and Hermes told Perseus to seek out the three Gray Women who lived in a cave at the foot of a huge mountain. They knew the way to the Gorgons and to the Stygian Nymphs—if he could find a way to make them tell him. "The Nymphs will prove good friends," advised Athena. "Be sure to seek them out before you try to kill Medusa."

When Perseus tracked down the Gray Women, he was shocked. They were ancient hags who shared one eye and tooth between them. Moving like a ghost, he crept behind their thrones and awaited his chance. As one passed their single eye and the tooth to another, Perseus leaped out. He seized the eye and tooth, leaving the women blind and squealing with rage. "If you want these back, tell me the way to the Nymphs and to the Gorgons' hiding place," he ordered. Helpless, they had no choice but to tell Perseus everything.

The Old Ones

The Gray Women were also known as the Graeae or Old Ones because their hair was gray from birth. Even so, in some myths they are described as swanlike and beautiful rather than ugly and frightening.

Ask the storyteller

Who were the Gray Women?

The Gray Women were sisters of the Gorgons. Their names were Enyo (warlike), Pemphredo (wasp), and Deino (terrible).

We'll tell you whatever you want to know.

The Stygian Nymphs

The Stygian Nymphs welcomed Perseus kindly and gave him three gifts—tools for his battle with the Gorgons. The first gift was a pair of winged sandals, like those worn by Hermes himself. The second was a magical helmet, called the Cap of Darkness, and the last, a silver *kibisis*, or pouch. Putting on the sandals, Perseus laughed in delight—they gave him the power of flight.

Thanking the Nymphs, he soared into the sky like a falcon seeking its prey. The Gray Women had told him that Medusa lived in the Land of the North Winds, Hyperborea. After a long journey, Perseus landed near the Gorgons' lair. He shuddered at what he found. All around him were the bodies of men and beasts turned into stone by the malevolent gaze of Medusa. Remembering Athena's warning, Perseus fixed his eyes on the reflection in his shield and warily began his attack.

The Cap of Darkness

The Cap of Darkness had a famous past. In the famous Trojan War between Greece and Troy, the goddess Athena herself fought on the side of the Greeks. When she first went into battle, she was wearing the magical cap.

Ask the storyteller
What powers did the other gifts bring?

Together with the flying sandals, the Nymphs gave Perseus other vital equipment. The Cap of Darkness made the wearer invisible, and the silver pouch changed size to hold whatever was put inside it.

17

Perseus Faces Medusa

Luckily for Perseus, the Gorgons were asleep, and he was able to creep in among the hideous sisters. Using the shield, he identified Medusa and took aim with the crystal sword. "Steady now," he whispered to himself, "you won't get a second chance." But his aim was true, and with one fierce blow, Perseus beheaded his foe. Bending to pick up her writhing head, he thrust it in the pouch. The serpents hissed in outrage as the darkness closed over them.

The next seconds were a whirl of horror. Perseus didn't know it, but Medusa was pregnant with the god Poseidon's children. As she died, she gave birth to a winged horse, Pegasus, and Chrysaor the warrior, armed with a golden sword. Wailing at the fate of their mother, the newborns woke their aunts, Stheno and Euryale. Suddenly, the odds looked grim, and Perseus turned to flee.

The Gorgons' lament

Athena had a cruel sense of humor. She heard Stheno and Euryale grieving over the death of Medusa and gleefully invented the flute to imitate the sound. Athena gave this new instrument to humans and called it "the music of many heads."

Hisss

Hisssss

Hisss

Hisss

Ask the storyteller

How did Perseus escape?
Perseus couldn't kill Stheno and Euryale, so he had to run—or rather fly—for his life. But the Gorgons flew after him. Perseus only escaped because he became invisible when he put on the Cap of Darkness.

The Curse of Atlas

Perseus headed south until strong winds blew him off course. He stopped to rest in the lands ruled by Atlas the Titan. Atlas was a god of immense strength whom no one dared to cross. A thousand herds of cattle roamed his pastures safe from bandits, while thieves stayed well away from his orchards of golden apples.

Perseus asked for a night's shelter and did his best to impress the Titan. "If noble family counts, I am the son of almighty Zeus." It was a boast best left unsaid. Atlas had been warned by an oracle that his apples would be stolen by a son of Zeus, his old enemy. "Away! Be gone!" the Titan ordered. "There is no welcome for you here."

Deeply insulted, Perseus wrestled with Atlas and pulled Medusa's head from the pouch. As the Titan stared into her dead eyes, he turned into the range of mountains—the Atlas Mountains—that still bears his name today.

Who was Atlas?

Atlas was a Titan, one of the older gods who ruled the earth before Zeus and the newer gods from Mount Olympus took over. Atlas led the Titans in a 10-year war against Zeus and only lost because the Cyclopes, one-eyed master craftsmen, made deadly weapons like Zeus's thunderbolts for the Olympians.

Get out, son of Zeus!

Ask the storyteller
What happened to Atlas?

In Greek mythology, Atlas is about as unlucky as you can get. He was singled out by Zeus for special punishment and ordered to hold the world on his back. After Perseus turned him into a mountain range, he still didn't get any rest. It is said that heaven rested on his peaks.

Andromeda and the Sea Monster

Perseus set out for home along the coast of Africa. Turning north across Philistia, he flew over a pitiful scene—a young woman chained to a sea cliff. Zooming down for a closer look, he saw that she was strikingly beautiful and fell instantly in love with her.

A wailing crowd stood on the beach nearby, and Perseus landed beside them. "Who is that girl?" he demanded. "Who dares treat her like this?" Her mother, Cassiopeia, and her father, Cepheus, stepped nervously forward. "We are the rulers of this land," they cried. "Poseidon, lord of the sea, has sent a monster to punish us. We have to sacrifice our daughter, Andromeda, to the beast—or we will all die." At once Perseus vowed to rescue Andromeda, and in return, her parents agreed that he could marry her and take her back to Greece.

Cassiopeia's boast

Queen Cassiopeia, like her daughter Andromeda, was very good looking. The queen had boasted that they were so attractive they even outshone the Nereids. This was a big mistake! The Nereids were beautiful mermaids, and they complained bitterly to Poseidon about this insult from a mere mortal.

Ask the storyteller

Why was Cepheus willing to sacrifice his daughter?

To punish Cassiopeia for being so vain, Poseidon sent a terrible sea monster to devastate Philistia. Cepheus had asked an oracle what he should do. He was told the only hope of saving his country was to feed his daughter to the monster.

Is anyone brave enough to save me?

The Jealousy of Agenor

Drawing his crystal sword, Perseus hovered over the sea, determined to stop the monster. However, as he dived down, the creature snapped at him and kept him away. Just in time, Perseus remembered he had the Cap of Darkness. As the serpent surged towards Andromeda, Perseus, invisible and undetected, struck a fierce blow and cut off its head.

Now that Andromeda was safe, Perseus unchained her and carried her ashore. Eager to marry her bold hero, Andromeda asked for the wedding to take place right away. The crowd cheered, and the celebrations had just begun, when Agenor arrived to break them up. He was Andromeda's old boyfriend and had come to claim her for himself—backed by an armed gang of more than 200 men. Perseus fought bravely. He beat Agenor, even though he was hopelessly outnumbered.

Set in the stars

Cassiopeia turned against Perseus as soon as the monster was dead. She said that he couldn't marry Andromeda because she was already engaged. Even worse, Cassiopeia sent a message to Agenor: "Come at once—Perseus must die!" To punish this betrayal, Poseidon set her picture in the stars. The constellation of Cassiopeia shows her tied up in a shopping basket.

Ask the storyteller

What happened to Agenor?

In the battle on the beach, Agenor was sure he would take Andromeda from Perseus. However, he didn't consider the contents in Perseus's pouch. With no other way to save himself and his bride, Perseus pulled out Medusa's head and turned Agenor and his gang into stone.

Where'd he go?

Perseus Rescues His Mother

Taking Andromeda with him, Perseus flew back to the island of Seriphos. He found his mother and was outraged to discover that Polydectes had lied. The king had tried to force Danae into marriage again. Perseus stormed into the palace to find Polydectes holding a banquet. "Here is a wedding present—the head of Medusa the Gorgon!" he announced, flinging down the pouch, only to be met with a chorus of jeers and insults from the king and his followers. "It's impossible to slay a Gorgon. You are a liar!" they yelled.

Wild with anger, Perseus reached into the pouch. Since no one believed he had killed Medusa, no one tried to stop him. Pulling out the dreadful head, he swung it in an arc around the room. Everyone who looked into the terrible eyes turned into a statue. Perseus turned and walked away, leaving the stone king and his petrified court in their frozen silence.

Refuge in the temple

Before the banquet, Danae and Dictys took refuge in a temple to escape Polydectes. There, they waited for Perseus to return. The king was frightened to drag them out in case he angered one of the gods. After Perseus had dealt with King Polydectes, he rewarded Dictys's loyalty to Danae by making him king of Seriphos.

What's he got in the...

Ask the storyteller

What happened to Medusa's head?

With his mother safe, Perseus's task was done. Athena gratefully accepted the head of Medusa as a gift and hung it on her shield. After this, the Gorgon's head became one of her symbols.

27

The Death of Acrisius

Perseus now looked forward to a quiet life. Together with his mother and Andromeda, he set sail for Argos. His grandfather, Acrisius, who had sealed him in the wooden chest so many years ago, heard of their return and fled to the city of Larissa.

Soon, however, Perseus was to follow him there by accident. He simply went to compete in the funeral games that the king of Larissa was holding in honor of his dead father. Perseus took part in the pentathlon, and when it came to throw the discus, he threw with all his strength and skill. But the wind sprang up, and the gods played with fate again. His discus blew off course and struck an old spectator, killing him instantly. To everyone's astonishment, the old spectator turned out to be Acrisius!

Fate catches up with Acrisius

Acrisius was terrified when he heard that Perseus was coming back to Argos. The oracle had foretold his death, and surely, the old man thought, his grandson was coming to kill him. Little did he know that Perseus had forgiven him and only wanted to become friends. Tragically, when Acrisius ran away, he set the scene for the oracle's prophecy to come true.

Ask the storyteller
How did Perseus feel?

Perseus was so ashamed that he had slain Acrisius that he couldn't face returning to Argos. Instead, he exchanged lands with his cousin, the king of Tiryns. Perseus ruled Tiryns for many happy years with Andromeda by his side.

A strong boy like that would make a father proud.

Glossary

Blacksmiths Metal workers.

Constellation A group of stars that make an image in the night sky.

Cyclopes One-eyed giants, who were also skilled at making things.

Epic A long poem about war and the deeds of heroes.

Immortal A being who cannot die, such as a god.

Kibisis A magical silver pouch that changes to hold what is put inside it.

Malevolent Wishing to do harm.

Mortal A being who will die one day, or who can be killed.

Nereid A nymph who lives in the sea.

Nymph A beautiful young woman related to the gods.

Olympus The home of Zeus and the other Olympian gods.

Oracle A person who can tell what will happen in the future.

Pentathlon An athletic event including five sports: running, javelin, discus, wrestling, and long jump.

Petrified Extremely frightened *or* turned into stone.

Philistia The land that is now modern Israel.

Prophecy A tale of what will happen in the future.

Temple A place of worship. Most gods had temples built in their honor.

Titans A set of gods who were overthrown by Zeus and the other gods of Olympus.

Who's Who

Acrisius (ah-KRISS-ee-us) King of Argos and grandfather of Perseus.

Agenor (uh-JEE-nor) Fiancé of Andromeda.

Andromeda (an-DROM-uh-da) Daughter of Cassiopeia and Cepheus.

Apollo (uh-POLL-o) God of medicine and music.

Athena (uh-THEE-nah) Daughter of Zeus and protectress of Athens.

Atlas (AT-luss) One of the Titans.

Cassiopeia (kass-ee-o-PEE-a) Mother of Andromeda and Queen of Philistia.

Cepheus (SEE-fee-us) Father of Andromeda and King of Philistia.

Chrysaor (kriss-AY-or) Son of Medusa.

Danae (DAN-eye) Mother of Perseus.

Dictys (DIK-tiss) A fisherman and brother of King Polydectes.

Euryale (you-ree-AH-lay) Sister of Medusa.

Hephaestus (hih-FES-tuss) God of blacksmiths.

Hermes (HER-meez) Son of Zeus and Maia and messenger for the gods.

Maia (MY-a) A goddess and mother of Hermes.

Medusa (med-OOS-ah) The Gorgon killed by Perseus.

Pegasus (PEG-uh-sus) The winged horse of Greek myth and son of Medusa.

Perseus (PURSE-ee-us) Son of Zeus and one of the most famous Greek heroes.

Polydectes (poll-ee-DEK-teez) King of Seriphos.

Poseidon (poss-EYE-don) God of the sea and brother of Zeus.

Proetus (PRO-tus) Brother of King Acrisius.

Stheno (STHEN-oh) A Gorgon sister of Medusa.

Zeus (ZOOS) King of the Greek gods.

Index